SLEEPING VOLCANO

a collection of poetry

by

Dubravka Velasevic

Hearing Eye

Published by
Hearing Eye,
Box 1,
99 Torriano Avenue,
London NW5 2RX

ISBN 1 870841 70 0

This publication has been made possible with the financial assistance of the London Arts Board.

Printed by Aldgate Press, London E1
Typeset by Daniel James at mondo designo
Cover design by Emily Johns

Dubravka Velasevic was born in Montenegro (Yugoslavia), where she practiced medicine and published two collections of poetry *Steep Gilding* (Belgrade 1996) and *Venetian Festivities* (Zagreb 1991). ⟶ *1986*

Since 1992 she has been living in London, where she at first translated some of her earlier work. For the last seven years she has been writing in English. Hearing Eye published her first collection of poetry in English, *Farewell Montenegro*, in 1996 (ISBN 1 870841 44 1).

In 1997 her collection *Departure* was published in Zagreb, Croatia (for which she translated *Elegies for My Mother* from the original English into her native language).

Her poetry is included in the following anthologies: *Regnbagens Sanger*, poetry of the former Yugoslavia (Symposium, Stockholm 1991); *Terra Mar E Lume*, South Slavonic poetry translated into Gallego (Hunta de Galicia 1996); *Home* edited by Kathleen McPhilemy (Katabasis, London 2000).

CONTENTS

I

The smile of the miracle

II

Voices

III

Elegies for My Mother

INTRODUCTION

Sleeping Volcano is an extraordinary collection of poems by a truly remarkable person. Dubravka Velasevic, already a revered poet in her native Montenegro and a successful doctor (though still only in her early thirties), was suddenly swept up by the convulsions brewing in Yugoslavia — and if not actually forced, she was certainly strongly induced by events there to leave for Britain in 1992. She had grown up in the town of Titograd, a warm, lush area between sea and mountains where relationships among the various ethnic groups had been untroubled, and in the midst of a loving extended family.

I first met Dubravka at a meeting of the English Centre of PEN. She had been a member of PEN in Montenegro and, indeed, was to represent that country at several international congresses after her move to Britain. She had learned English at school, but her speech was still hesitant in the living, ever-changing tongue. Nevertheless, within a few years, she bravely took on the challenge of translating her own poems from the Serbo-Croatian.

I felt privileged to be asked to read the manuscript for a pamphlet she was preparing for Hearing Eye, *Farewell Montenegro*. We talked about certain words and their precise and colloquial meanings, and I was amazed at her grasp of nuance; how she could, in fact, handle double meanings to create mystery and irony in English. The poems, simple on the surface, had an eerie depth to them, like the proverbial 'still waters.'

But Velasevic was to dare even more. She began writing new poems directly in English. And the new work did not retreat into imitative forms, but developed almost seamlessly in rhythms that continued to reflect the emotional cadences gleaned from Southern and Eastern European culture, her admiration, for instance, for the Russian poet, Marina Tsvetaeva, who was a great influence, and for whom she has written a memorable 'Requiem.'

Velasevic has returned several times on visits to Montenegro — visits fraught with anxiety and even danger. Sadly, she has attended funerals there: her mother's, her grandmother's. She is very attached to her family, and her love for them imbues her poetry with a filial devotion rare in English, most notably in the final section of this book, the beautiful 'Elegies for My Mother.'

Dubravka Velasevic's poems are, indeed, all about love — of people, of landscape, of the world she has left behind and the world she would have it become again. Her poetry enriches not only the English language but also the English-speaking soul with a music that is at once exotic and yet altogether familiar in the depths of our common humanity.

Leah Fritz

THE END OF AN ERA

'This is the end of an era'
My personal horoscope says

What does it mean I wonder
'Oh, yes!'

My grandmother's dying silence
The death of a long-lost childhood
The innocence

It seems as if the whole world is vanishing:
The fig trees
The cyclamen clusters
The leaves on the frozen branches
The cracked walnuts
Myths and fairies

The pictures are dying in my memory
The smells
The light of dawn in the cypress trees

This is definitely the death
Of the age I knew best
Of so many years taken for granted
A change of what I used to call 'my old self'

The faded voices of the past
The names
Vanishing from the list of friends
So many towns flattened
The burnt gates

This really looks like The End
Of a life chapter

Youth's ephemeral rest
Mortality's conquest

EXTRATERRESTRIAL

I walk around
dressed in innocence

I refuse to use
spectacles for ugliness
senses for abhorrence

I refuse to listen
to anything
except the beauty of the Universe

I breathe easiness
and Godlikeness

I eat only
vibrant colours of leaves

And sleep only
in the rain forests of Brazil

I dream only
of the coastline of Atlantis

Of the sea waves
bathing the gold and silver beaches

And I sit only
under palm trees

Feeding coconuts to elves
strawberries to fairies

I swim only
in dream waters
of forest green nakedness

In the transparency of sunlight
reflecting from the pyramids

Yes, I have a confession to make

I am an extraterrestrial
from this planet!

I am a dream's web
dreaming itself

A loud sigh
of the forest's arch

A deep afternoon's shade
A mystery of rivers

And a stream's giggle
where nymphs come down
to sing
and to gather

Yes, I have a confession to make
I am the Universe itself

A God's shepherdess
guarding day

I wear stars
instead of gloves
Using the Milky Way
as my path

What can I say about the winds?
I have a great respect for them

But I am a fan of the light breeze
and the Spring in my hair

I admire stone
Karst
and crags

I love rocks above the seashore
worshipping the pale morning light

I am addicted to dawn
to the colours of dusk

Sun-fanaticism
My only weakness

Otherwise
No dark secrets

THE SMILE OF THE MIRACLE

How much wasted time
How many wasted years
Even youth has quietly vanished
Waiting for that miracle's smile

How many poems never written
How many plays never performed
How many letters I've never sent
How many days never enjoyed

So much unrecognised treasure
So many extinguished rubies
So many hours when I was late
So much darkened gold

How many sunken lands of Atlantis
How many undiscovered reincarnations

Hurry up!
Quickly!
Now

This life — won't last for ever

AFTER VISITING CRNOJEVIC RIVER

That mist rising above the water
seemed so unreal

In which language can I describe
the feeling of something supernatural

I expected nymphs
I expected gnomes
forest-green fairies
and other nature spirits
to materialise that evening
on the shore of Crnojevic River

Spattered with the summer shower
merging with the wildness of the hills
Crnojevic River looked beautiful but dead
like most Montenegrin dreams

The mountains were squatting in Lake Skadar
The water lilies growing dimmer
as night came visiting again

Every time I tried to capture
the image of the lake
the photo in my mind
would immediately fade

Why is it
that I cannot take with me
the pictures so precious
for my mental world
for my artist's eye?

Why do I have to leave behind
Places I belong to
Beauty I live on?

Everything I love

POMEGRANATES
(for my grandmother Milica)

I think often of that day
when I was only eighteen
and you were already grey

I remember you standing on the doorstep
of your country house
Sky heavy with the coming rain
Autumn pregnant
Fresh magic in the air

How warm
how comforting
was your country house
smelling of that early autumn dampness
The cupboards full of pomegranates

The wine fermenting in the cellars
A few remaining grapes
in already yellow fields

The vineyards with hardly any leaf on them
going bald and songless
The delicate oak-forests
dressed in orange silk

Grandmother,
You always waited on the doorstep
like one of those Guardian Angels
whenever you heard approaching steps

Your country house
since my early childhood
was one of those fairy tale castles

With 'rooms with a view'
and those high windows
where I sat for hours
staring at the summers
and the meadows

My early poems written there
were full of intense passion
Mad love
Obsessions

I didn't know at the time
that passion was a nightmare
A poison to stay away from

But that October day
my mood was quiet and a happy one
The world seemed to stand still
It happens sometimes when you are very young

For a moment
time didn't seem to matter
My restlessness was absent

Inhaling the sweetness of the Earth
I felt immortal
I felt powerful

That day — taken out of Paradise
Held such peace and bliss

With you, grandmother,
Abiding elsewhere now

In memories

PROUD TO BE FOREIGN

I have never belonged anywhere anyway...

I did not need to be called
either 'this' or 'that'
in order to have known
who I was
or who I am

I have never belonged anywhere anyway...

The only certain thing about me was —
that I came to life on this planet

Even in my country I was as foreign
as anywhere else

To be called Yugoslav, Etruscan, or Montenegrin
It didn't really matter
It never truly defined
either my name
or my essence

I suppose
I was born foreign
to most of the places and things

For I have never belonged anywhere anyway...

SLEEPING VOLCANO

Leave that volcano to sleep

For I can smell the fire
Trying to untangle the handcuffs
To escape through the skin

Let's keep that volcano asleep

For the beast is never really innocent
And neither of us are
Beyond the great danger
If you release the steam

Leave that dragon undisturbed
For they can start to roar:
The earthquakes
The hurricanes
Amazons

Let them safely sleep
Away in the distant past
In the long forgotten myths

For somehow I know —
Before is always better
Than what comes after the sorrow

Leave that volcano to dream

For I can see the ashes
Falling down from the mountains
Turning spring into greyness
The verdure of the valleys
Into darkness

So you had better leave that volcano to sleep

THAT VOLCANO WITHIN ME...

Oh, that Volcano,
That Volcano within me!

I have such difficulty
To keep it asleep

To secure the guards
The chains — tight enough
To prevent the outbursts of troublesome passion
Those eruptions of love

Oh, that Volcano,
That Volcano deep within me!

It's so hard
To prevent it exploding

I wrestle with it
Day and night

Even when I dream
'He' is awake
And so much alive

Oh, that Volcano,
That Volcano within me!

How blessed are those ones
With tiny fires smouldering within

Instead of this threatening heat
Raging in my heart

OFFERING

'I bring you lots of beauty' I said
'Will you see to it?
Will you harvest it?'

And you said:
'How wonderful!
What a gift.
What a pity!
I cannot feed on it
I cannot drink it.'

'I bring you lots of Love' I said
'Will you love me then?
Will you, will you?
Will you live with me for ever?'

And you, startled:
'I love you!
I love your love
I love being loved by you.
I will always treasure this feeling
This miracle'

'I have brought you lots of cherries' I said
'And bees
And honeysuckle
Lots of gold
And lots of rings

Will you have them then?
Will you paint my lips into cherry-red?

Will you sweeten this bitterness of nights
This loneliness of winters?

Will you decorate with gold
These sunlit autumn mornings
And my naked fingertips?'

DREAMLAND

Oh,
How much I missed you
How much I missed your hand!

I missed you
Even when I was with you
Didn't you know that?

Your eyes were so dreamlike
Why can't you say 'I'll go ahead!'

Life has stopped for far too long
The sky is blooming
Get yourself ready
Don't wait!

Yes, they are still screaming —
Those sweet teddy-bears
About the damage they'd like to mend

But why not say 'No' to the past's ghosts
And join the feast of the land

Why not forgive
And let go

It's a waste to be alive
But scared

And Anger...
What to do with the anger?

You say 'It's nice.
But it pains'

If the anger was worth so long searching for
We all would be by now long dead

Sleep well, my friend!

Let farewell be silent

The Greek isles cannot stand
The sadness of the constant partings

I'll see you — in my dreamland

You'll find me — on your hand

MELANCHOLY

When that melancholy reaches me—
It happens always in twilight—
My restlessness becomes unbearable
Me and my past—growing apart

Then I pick up the phone and ring
People from the past
It's like ringing zombies

The voices distant
Stone-like
The emotions shattered
Silent cries

That reflection in the mirror
I search for—
It's not there any more
Only an emptiness
Only an echo

When that melancholy gets hold of me
Like some maniac in the dawn
I cannot escape feeling exposed
To all the winds around the world

My past as real as my dreams
Of round time
Sleeping with nymphs

When that melancholy has a crush on me
I feel more vulnerable than the sea
Ridden by storms of angry Poseidon

The past is gone
And it's not there

As if I'd had just a brief love-affair
With myself

And nothing else

OCTAGONAL STARS
(for a Chinese girl)

The darkness you came from
Who knows what it contained...
A carbon,
Or chrome?

Behind your glance
There were shadows in the meadows
Where night mingles
With nightingales
And crows

That loss of memory
Almost amnesia
For the childhood tyranny
The filth and septicaemia

Octagonal and pentagonal stars
Were so darkened in your country
By those clouds of cruelty
The knives of karma

And that lack of ability to laugh
At such seriousness of life
Which seemed to be a constant search
A constant march

At the end of the tunnel
There was fading light

That other world in your eyes
The secrets
The numbness

Almost — a death of a smile

And you — you are doing so well
Your speeches bravado style
Hiding the hurt behind the shrewdness
Doing so well behind the Chinese mask

I ALWAYS WANTED...

I always wanted a daughter
Someone pink and white
With blue eyes

Everything that wasn't me:
A pale face
My dark ancient eyes
My dark hair in restless waves
Melancholy twilights

Maybe
I wanted myself

Just in a different shape

POEMS ON THE TRAIN

When I sit on the train
Poems come

Embarrassed
I start a search for a pen

Not to miss
The glint of light

The whisper from the Goddess

SANTORINI

That day full of rage, fire and God's grace
All unforgettable lives visited me page by page
On what was once Atlantis
Such a divine place

Against the view of steep blackened hills
The burnt out past came back to me
Straight from the crystal libraries

I thought 'I must stay this time
For the volcano is still alive
Half-asleep in the burning air'

I discovered
I was still in love with the island
After so many lives of a different kind

When I entered the sea
It was like a christening of unknown me

I felt I was the Aegean sea
Following its rhythm in my skin

Atlantis,
Why did the gods get so angry with you?

It must have been some terrible sins
Which outshone your deadly charm
And your more than exquisite beauty

Or—maybe you were sacrificed
To a raging Neptune
One night when he was very drunk

But did you cry?

For I could hear no echo of your grief

As if all the tears
Had turned into gold and myths

AUSTRALIA POEM I

I wore the smile of the Indian Ocean
on my skin
The gentle touch of the white sandy beach
The closeness of Norfolk pine trees

I smiled at the afternoon
Sipped the afternoon tea

Under the shade of a constant search
for something else outside
and something more within

I did not like that Lapsang Souchong taste —
too smoky for my lips

I preferred to stay within the glare
of those distant eucalyptus trees

I liked the kangaroos though
the sweetest of all beasts

While emus were parading
their long necks and pointed heads
Like extraterrestrials
too real for the sunsets

Australia, forgive me!
I didn't know what to expect

Certainly not the miracle
I found waiting there

AUSTRALIA POEM II

That beach made me beautiful
That full moon dazzled me

The eucalyptus wood made me realise
The illusion of poetry

I caught the sun on my face —
The sun glare from Heaven

Like overfeeding the hunger
Or overwatering the desert

That full moon made them beautiful —
The snow of the dunes

I needed two pairs of sunglasses
To face the beauty of the world

WE FILLED THAT ROOM WITH OUR PRESENCE

I

We filled that room with our presence
It wasn't meant to be empty
Loneliness wasn't on purpose

The day was the finest spring one
I could almost say 'perfect'
Light — pale and cool
The birds dreaming my dreams
In their own world

I was wondering where to go next?

That spring desire for departing
took hold of me once again
But all the desires have been already explored
You had better find some peace!
Otherwise, let's go!

II

Some boring person in front of my gate
was competing with the snails
painting the house walls for days

Someone next door
was suffering an attack of spring overjoy
playing music until almost the dawn

Celebrating something?
You would do better
to go dancing naked in the fields
Or to run alongside rivers in the mist

But where to find fields in this urban scenery?
A shortage of country idyll
is so painfully real!

III

And I started writing a funny kind of poetry
Not my style at all!

Maybe London was interfering
with my subconscious
or my soul ?

London — the second best place in the world to be
if you are not in your native country
My homeland lost in obscured memory

IV

As I said earlier:
'I am not a midnight type of a lady at all!
I am much more of a morning lady indeed'

As for me, night could go away for ever
I wouldn't miss it!
I wouldn't miss it!
I would feel no regret and no pity

V

Had I been living in Ancient Egypt
I would have gone every dawn
to the temple of Amon Ra
to worship the Sun
to celebrate the light

But here I am in this mysterious land
of many winds
of dragging mists

I would have gone instead
to Stonehenge
To catch the dawn at solstice
to pray to the Sun
to revitalise me

VOICES

There was a word
And I did not write it down

It marked me with its smile
And perished
As miraculously as it had arrived

There was a poem
And I did not open my lips

The sound has never reached the brink

The arms of the sleeper
Never moved from the bier

There was a music
But the crowd's buzzing was louder

In the end
Nothing happened
To disturb the stillness of the ether

AN OLIVE TREE IN THE HEAT OF A JULY MIDDAY
(for Richard McKane)

A serpent-like tree
The trace of time carved on it

The emptiness of the ancient jars
The broken sound of amphorae

Mocking the haze of a July midday
The lusty glances of the passers by

There stands
Like a scornful nymph

That gracious olive tree

VENETIAN NIGHT

A pure innocence
A blessing from the darkness
I request!

In the cold silence of cathedrals
In the hot sun of alkazars
A sheer misplacement dreaming
Enigmas' illusory longing

A poignant debauchery of the stone
Out of the flame alone
The echo of the carving came so remote
The dust above the water still floats

The silk was drowning the dusk
The treacherous phantoms of the past
The sun paved by the lust

What kind of mood
Is this mood of mine,
So sombre tonight?

In these grimy Venetian waters
In the saddest of all evenings
It's pointless to start weeping

VENETIAN FESTIVITIES
(while listening to the music of André Campra)

Dead Venetian water
Ruptured consciousness of the horns
Murmuring the intrigues of the past

Magic or insolence
Falcon above its nest

Muted ghosts of the canals
Protracted parade of the night

Even the walls became decayed
Because of too much power, alas!

The marvellous suite has gone
The guests in the drizzle of the masks

In the harlequin's dress it disappeared
That kingdom of flattery and lust

PHANTASM

Between you and me
Steel threads are sparking

Opal
Gold desire

Agate
Milky doors

Between the two of us
There is an inner voice

The passion tempts the skin
The soul burns in the eyes

Between me and you
Boats wander and barcaroles float

Between you and me
Dreams and riddles
Hard teeth of comets
Holy embraces

Between you and me
Gentle links are flowing

Cosmic
Fervent phantasms

Pain
And steep beauty of risk

ON THE PALM OF THE WINDS

Shattered by time
Burdened by night

Martyred by the elusiveness
Of mornings

Dispersed
By the ambrosia of dreams

Tired of sorrow
Blinded by desire for tomorrow

Swallowed
With the nectar of the Gods

Iphigenia
On the palm of Aeolus

LAMENT OF THE PILLARS OF AN ANCIENT TEMPLE

Side by side
Under the winged sky
Forever separated
By this stony arch

We grew up
In the absence of touch
We opened our hearts
To that north light

Oh my brother,
Who has come
From the same roots
And the same blood

I swear to you on these crags
Whence we have sprung into life
Into this melancholy WHY

That we'll find a consolation
In the closeness of our bodies
For they could have planted us out
In two different countries

Even beside you
I feel so lonely
By the savage wind
I am eaten away
The temple's rigour captured my flame

They carved my hands
Engraved this image with no voice
So, I must listen to anonymous prayers
Until the day of apocalypse

My stony brother, so exposed
To the glances of the passing hordes
My breath keeps you whole

We are two blades
In the same sheaf of grass

Waiting—reunited in the mystery of night

My brother in art
Existence and lust

Have we found ourselves
On this spiritual path?

ZEUS' CHARIOT

Over there
Behind hearing
In the well of the secret of the brain
The winds howl and the wild beasts stare

Hydra
Seducing the games of death
The masts of the sunken ships
Ghostly roofless castles
Swaying in the air

Over there
Beyond sight
Hidden from every eye
Phantom Atlantis parades through the night

Over there
Beyond pain and scent
The sparrows still tug Zeus' chariot

Over there
Somewhere in tiers
The still present past — so near

FEAST or ABOUT LOVE
(according to Plato's 'Symposium')

Nothing links us any more
Deserted roads
And empty corridors

Walked-out
Washed-out milky paths
Which once led
Through the battlefields
Of our hearts

Rusty river bridges
Won't be raised again
No creak of chains
The teeth won't grind
In an agony of pleasure

Frosty glances of cold hands
Cannot reach you any more
Stalactites of kisses
Grow into the wilderness of dawn

Who could foresee us
Happily separated
Returned to ourselves
In the nick of time?

Long ago
Caravans and winds
Stopped travelling through those fields

The petals of sand
Do not bloom here any more

It's been long time
Since anyone set off
For this desert of the soul

And maybe there was nothing
From the very beginning

Except an evening gloom
And the desire for time to go

Maybe we just fooled ourselves:
Body by body
Mind by mind
Spying on the night

Two worlds
Two holy systems of the brain

An unweeded basket
Of Biblical strain

Nothing links us any more
Deserted doorsteps
And empty floors

Who ever accomplished Plato's task
Of putting together
Two apple halves?

SNAKE'S WHISPER

My teeth are silent
My bite so harmless

My poison sobers up
Your darkest thoughts
Become white

Your perception is wrong
You malicious man!

In the softness of death
In the silence of dream
I shall plunge your fears

With a sting towards tranquillity
With a knife over the knots of hope
Through the narcosis to the eternity

It takes just a second

Not more than two

DARK AS THE NIGHT

Someone
Dark as the night which brings bad news
A black hole for his soul
Hungry as a greyhound after a futile hunt
He crept into my secret thoughts
Plunging my senses into chaos

Someone
With a dusky voice
His eyes glowing like an oil lamp
His hands promising bliss
He uncovered the flame in the core of darkness
With gold chains he conquered my restlessness

Someone
Dark as a thunder in the inflamed wind
He almost turned into stone
Inside my throat

That someone
Sunless in his soul
So dark
And so alone

GLITTERING OF THE FIRE

I can feel here inside
hurricanes
legions
smiles
always storming in advance

A tide close to suffering
A green fire's glittering

I can feel how
with the salty noble sword
you dissolved the reality's cord

Among the peaks of the wild beasts
squinting on the mountains
Among Bacchus's sleepless escorts
in front of the temple
love will call

And then
the night will wake up
in spite of a lullaby
The sound of a mighty silence
will conceive a divine presence

Among the tongues of the green stones
a flash of breasts
and the dawn

Can't you feel behind the cliffs
whispering sirens
calling Odysseus

Will the walls fall down
if the legions shout?

When daybreak overhead
is born again
And we think it is a comet

But, it's not!
It is difficult and hot

Maybe the depth of the Red Sea
will open again its ancient secrets
for the column of light
to pass by

And then the silent ebbing
will gently wrinkle the sea's surface
Without a sign of storms
shipwrecks
barcaroles

And the sea will be
calm
and holy

So will my desire
my soul
and my body

THE SONG OF AN EMPTY JAR

I carry proudly my emptiness
Through the world
A small grain of a forgotten Universe

A silky womb
Suckled on a darkness
The seriousness of the commenced day
The thundering comprehensiveness of repentance

I do not swagger with a cold reality
With the inherited silence
With a clay inaccessible to the eyes' vanity

Come closer!
Have a look!

The depths of the mirrors
Still remember you

THE ISLAND

Around — the silence
Around — the emptiness

The sight merges with infinity
The womb cries out of pity

The sunken ships keep mute cunningly
The masts nowhere to be seen

The shells ingratiate themselves with the sea
The land with no sign of footprints

A prayer to the silent birds
The echo of your secret thoughts

You can never reach
Another island

The most distant star
Seems so much closer

THE MIST

I flung myself in the mist
Mumbling prayers

The mist welcomed me
With cutting edges
With forks
With pliers

I clenched my teeth
And plunged my hands
Into the trunk of the willow tree

A decayed forest
Silenced the lament

Curse!
Spit!
Discourage!

The trees of blessings
Will arise again

DEAD OF NIGHT

Tonight you should tell
All about yourself
To the stone deaf faces
Of the ash trees

Along eerie streets
Whitened with confusion
You should thrust yourself
In the mouth of the full moon

The darkness is complete

You nibble the chaos of the night
While you rest on the abyss
Your unaccustomed sight

The challenge of the stars
A pace towards the past

Once like that he lay —
Hector before Troy
In the silent clotted dark

REQUIEM FOR MARINA TSVETAEVA

It has been a long time
Since she was gone
Resting in the darkness of aeons

As if she had never stepped
Into the dawn
Marina she was called
Like a sea-stone

Wrapped in the icy chains
Of sadness and despair
She has been sleeping for decades
In a proud solitude of a poet

Only her green and grey eyes
Still burn in twilight

Marina's rhyme — so alive

Where did you go so alone?
Shutting the doors behind you

Escaping the world's darkness
You, uncrowned princess of stubbornness

You gilded the dust
With your 'white heart'
With that desperate fall
Of comets and meteors

You still sing about yourself
However dead

And your rhyme, Marina, is so alive!
In the vastness of the Russian night

WAITING FOR THE WHITE BIRD

For days and days
I have been waiting for the white bird
To start silvering in the view
Like bronze scales in the sea-silence

For days and days
I have been fighting my hesitance:
'It will come. It will not —
That mythical bird with the heart of gold'

In the ecstasy of the womb
A desire resonates so strong
While fishing nets keep dreaming
The eternal rest

The horizon for days
Has been covered in purple sunsets
Full of rocks
And mermaids' laments

Obscured by such strong desire
You cannot see far enough

And I do not want
To finish this song

My sixth sense says 'It will come one day!'
That white bird — a boat in an open sea
Misleading trails
Under the deck of destiny

That bird with a divine throat
Galaxies are its wings

Yes, I keep waiting for the white bird
To make port in the nearest harbour

All my senses say 'It will come one day...'

I know
But, when?

MOURNING THE WAR
(addressed to all the criminals of the war 1991-1995
...in former Yugoslavia)

Night descended upon their fathers
And buried them
Under the autumn hatred
Their eyes closed themselves

The pain rolled
Through galleries of blood
And solitude

An ancient curse
Reaches out to generations to come

They sprinkled them
With the wine of Judgement Day
From the Holy Grail
They did not taste fate

Midnight fell upon them
Ultimate night
As if they had not believed
The Sun would rise again

Long ago
They stumbled into shame

God, forgive us for our sins!
Save us from ourselves
From evil thoughts
And evil acts!

Lord, look upon their hands
Splattered with crimson from the sunset

Hear the breathlessness of this hour
The sighing tears of our Saint

Give us light and holiness
In this vast loneliness!

Restore their reason
Which they lost on their journey
To sombre landscapes

Erase the bruises and the thorns
From the crown of your Son
And our God

Dispel demonic forces
Above these waters
And let the rivers run green again

Let the murderer return unharmed
To find at home:
An open door
A shattered hearth
Ashes in his bed

Let them not forgive themselves
For the rest of their lives
Let them curse their karma
And let them pray
In a deep self-regret

Your poor souls in blindness
Your poor eyes in ignorance

Even the ground moans
For you raped it
And maltreated it

A womb is weeping
For you crawled out of it
Like poisonous vipers in the early spring

You are an error
In the divine script
Nothing human about you
But the darkness in the crypt

ELEGIES FOR MY MOTHER

ONE

Mother,
At that last moment
You called my name

As if I could prevent
The storming death
That swept you away

I feel
I betrayed
Your ultimate request

TWO

Mother,
I eat my food
And drink my drink

And you,
You cannot eat
You cannot drink
Because there is nothing there

No room
For earthly pleasures

THREE

Mother,

I feel
I could get drunk tonight

On this grief

Not
The wine

FOUR

If there is reincarnation
I want to meet you again

You might tell me the things
Only you knew

But never said

FIVE

Ashamed
When I start my dinner

I think of you
Asleep in Heaven

SIX

On the day of your funeral
I asked
I prayed:

'Mother,
If your soul is somewhere around
Please give me a sign
Let bird sing
Let cock crow'

At first
An absolute silence

Then
When they were putting
The coffin with your body
Into the grave

The birds
In a nearby cypress tree
The cock
In some courtyard
Started singing

Went mad

SEVEN

Mother,

I still ring home
And expect

You'll pick up the phone
And tell me

You are not dead

EIGHT

Why do I think
There were so many things
I wanted to tell you
To whisper to your face

An unfinished dialogue
Is staring at me

A conversation with the silence

NINE

Oh, Mother,
Mother,

This emptiness
In the space

This time
Lacking your presence

It seems unbearable

So hard to face

TEN

I grieve
And grieve

It doesn't help
It doesn't go away

It seems
I cannot escape

The memory of that last surprise
On your dying face

ELEVEN

Mother,
I love you!

Though you don't exist any more
On this earthly plane

I love you, my dearest,
Wherever you are
In those vast nameless maps
Of galaxies
And shooting stars

I loved you, Mother,
More than I loved anyone

TWELVE

I cry
And cry

And then remember
How brave you were

And never liked tears

I try to smile

THIRTEEN

Seven days without you
Seven days

What will seven years be like

With you hiding
Behind seven veils

FOURTEEN

Mother,

It hurts
It hurts so much
It doesn't go away

I never knew
It would be this painful

Your death

Your departure

FIFTEEN

Oh, Mother,
My loving Mother!

I miss you!
I miss you!

I want to shout

To let you know how much
I long to see you

This moment

Right now

SIXTEEN

I want to talk to you
To your soul

I beg you
Give me a sign
A call from above

I still love you

You must know that

Wherever it is you now hide

SEVENTEEN

Oh, my dear Mother!

How much I miss you
On the buses
On the Underground
That you were never on

How often I see you
In my mind

And hardly an hour passes by
When I don't think of you

I still can't accept
The sadness of your departure

EIGHTEEN

Mother,
I love you!
I love you!

Can't you hear?
Can't you answer back?

I love you my dearest!

You must sense that

NINETEEN

My beloved Mother,
My dear,

Where are you?
Where are you?

Somewhere far

Or somewhere near

TWENTY

I want to say a 'Farewell' to your soul
After the forty days of wandering around

Travel in peace!
On your journey to God

May the angels be by your side
To protect you from all the fears
Of unknown sights

May you rest in peace!
And in light!

Forget all the pain
You suffered in this life

Remember the Love
And all the beauty of this world
However small
Insignificant
And temporary its shelter for you once was

Travel in peace!
To wherever your soul is to go
After the forty days of wandering alone

Travel, my beautiful
Once and forever Mother!

Go!

Don't wait!

Join the others!

TWENTY-ONE

I guess
That Greek Orthodox music
Reminded you of death

That's why, I think,
You refused to have it played

And I naively thought
It will bring you a consolation
The promise of eternal life
Free of any threat

Forgive me, oh Mother,
For the lack of wisdom
In your final days!

TWENTY-TWO

Even after three months
Almost every night
You come into my dreams
Dead but still alive

Oh, Mother!
Please tell me
What is this all about?

A joy
As well as torture
Of seeing you at night

I can't ever kiss you
I can't give you a hug

For
You are never really dead

But never alive enough

TWENTY-THREE

Mother,
You came again last night

You were lying down
As you do
In most of my dreams

I knew you were not alive
But you could move
And you could speak

I felt
Such heaviness in my heart
Such a grief

Did you want to tell me something?
A message
From the world you are now in

I can't remember
What you talked about
Last night
Exactly five months since you have died

But I know
I was puzzled again
For in my dream
Of course, you were not

But I was—alive

TWENTY-FOUR

Oh, Mother!

Who knows:
Which dreams
Which wishes
Desires
Ambitions

You carried to the grave
Silently with you

TWENTY-FIVE

More and more often
When I look in the mirror
I see your face, Mother,
God, let me live long!

In the morning
I recognise your features

While washing away my sleepiness
Like a ritual

Are you coming through me now, Mother?
Are you visiting my so-called reality?
No longer only my dreams?

Are we becoming one?
As, in a strange way, we always were

Like the double existence
Of twin sisters

Are you being born these days again, Mother?

Through the miracle of mirrors
Through the magic of unknown days

TWENTY-SIX

I suppose
I can write these elegies for you
For the rest of my life

For
You won't be coming back
From the other side

And I can wait
As long as I like

For you to appear
And to say:
'Here I am.
You didn't expect'

Just wishful thinking
I am afraid

TWENTY-SEVEN

Did someone tear off
A part of my being
The moment you died
The day you left

For I bent so heavily

Like a tree in the storm

Like somebody punched
In the abdomen

Like a pilgrim struck
By lightning
On a rainy day

TWENTY-EIGHT

'What will you do?'
I asked
'If you need help
When I go away?'

'There are other doctors
Who can cure me,
If I need them,
Don't be so vain' you said

And now —
You lie
Not cured but dead

And I carry my guilt
Like a cross
Through the rainbow of days

As slaves
Once carried
Their stony chains

TWENTY-NINE

THE FLAMES FROM THE TWO CANDLES IN THE CHURCH

That day
In the church
The flames from the two candles
Were talking to me

'I am your mother's soul' said the first
'Don't you recognise me?
Don't you know?

I greet you with this flickering light
So happy to see you again

The fire from your matches
Warms my heart
My bodiless existence'

'I am your grandmother's breath' said the second
'It used to be my birthday today
While I was still on the earthly plane

We are again a mother and a child

I was so sad
When my eldest daughter passed away
That I had to rush to find her
In that darkness beyond life

And now
We are two embraced lights
Somewhere really high

We speak beyond words
And see beyond eyes

And your mother is
Still my devoted daughter

Though no bodies
No weight
And no time exist
Where we have been transferred

Everything is floating
Everything transparent
Where we now are

But our love for you
Is still unchanged

And for ever alive'

THIRTY

I cried, Mother,
When I tasted that rakeeya
Made of the grapes from your vineyard
Under the burning Montenegrin sun

It was like being able to see you once again
To touch you
To hold on to your strength

I thought—
How kind of my uncle
To send me that bottle

So I could taste again the past
Sample days from my childhood

When tasting rakeeya
Or drinking a red wine

Seemed so natural
Seemed so wonderful

Like being alive

SPRING HYMN
(for my Mother)

I wanted to sleep
I wanted to dream

About you
Coming to see me

I refused to get up
I refused to wake up

I resisted opening my eyes

But once I did —
I saw the spring

Bathing in the sunlight
Singing ancient hymns

For a complete list of Hearing
Eye publications, please write
enclosing an SAE to:

Hearing Eye,
Box 1,
99 Torriano Avenue,
London
NW5 2RX

Alternatively, please visit the
Hearing Eye website at:

http://www.torriano.org